Optimistic Misery

Something lighthearted, endearing and romantic sunbathing in melancholy.

By: Peter Cherry

Written by Peter Cherry

Arranger: Peter Cherry

Director and Creator: Peter Cherry

Copy Editors/Editors: Kalisha D. Lemmitt-
Cherry, Peter Cherry

Graphic Designer: Peter Cherry

Cover Artwork Design: Peter Cherry

Interior Artwork and Design: Peter Cherry Publishing and
Copyrights and Trademarks by Angelic Reign, Inc. 2024

ISBN: 979-8-9902578-0-1

For adult literary consumption only.

"This book for grown people."

Table of Contents

Simple…8
Passed the Torch…9
Day Tripping…10
Older…11
Imperfectly…13
Love's Bad Luck…14
I'll Tell 'Ya…15
Our L's…17
Wanna Hear About It…18
Been There Before…20
Fickle Thing…21
Honestly…22
"Da Feels" …23
Perhaps…30
Shit I'll Tell Ya…32
Say There… 35
Drop Down…3
What They Want, "That" …38
Hit My Music…39
She Chimed Back…41
Fool Heart…42
Same 'Ol…44
Love For Sale …45

Banter Present…47

Party Y'all…48

The DJ's Inner Mission…49

She Said That…51

Can You Match My Love...52

Esmeralda's Parasol…53

Weirdo...55

Got Hip…57

Forgotten Cups…59

Not Prepared…61

Struggle Love…63

Messy Note…65

Challenge 101…66

Take a Pic…68

Liquify…69

Dance Floor…70

Que Sera…73

Funk Me, Please…74

Emotion Sensors…75

Dark Clouds…76

"At The Club Notion Noir" …77

Fault False…82

Ideology…83

Too Late?...84

Sado Pussy Cat...85

She Told Me...87
She Asked...I Got Condoms...88
The Shake Dancer...89
On the Dresser...90
Tripping...91
Don't Waste My Time...92
I Love to Like You...93
Sparking Conversation...94
Undivided Attention...96
Silk and Lace...98
Wanna Funk...101
Pen Drifting...103

Shy Blush...104
Personalities Vines...105
Most News...106
Sometimes...107
Every Day Super...108
My Star...109
No Secret...110
Effort...111
Changing Things...112
Sensual Play...113
Naughty...114
Thaw in Passion...115
Good & Good...116
"Time and Attitude" ...117

Age of Wine …121
Original Artwork:
'Speaker Park' by Peter Cherry
(Peter Cherry, 2024) …122
A Letter to the Reader (Peter Cherry, 2024)…123
Picture of Peter Cherry (Peter Cherry, 2024)…124
Opportunity (Peter Cherry, 2024)…125
IN TUNE (Peter Cherry, 2024)…126
Out the Mud (Peter Cherry, 2024)….127

Simple

As hard as I try, and sometimes
I seldom do, I just can't
escape the presence and
the essence; just the ooh of you.
Slow dancing within a notion that is you,
or, is it just the motion of adore just admiring?
Sometimes,
slow dancing in a daydream can leave me spinning
and smoking like a locomotive. Question?
Is love just a convenience, or a conquest of
our notion of a blissful beautiful?
Answer.
Boastfully, both are true.
It's the desire and time, or maybe
I'm graciously losing my mind.
My rose petal love, surrounded by
lavender kisses of erotic thoughts,
when feelings occur, what is your initial reaction?
Where was love?
Was it within me, or, just like the beginning of the
sonnet, just admiring?

Passed the Torch

I admit,
I still love you;
but,
I'm not digging you right now.
They say love can be complicated, and
you're surely showing me right now.
I'm trying to understand it but
I just don't know how.
I've been in love; my heart been
broken; my feelings been bruised.
Yet, I still keep on going.
The emotion is acknowledged as it keeps on flowing;
knowing of self is an elephant;
never awkwardly showing; overwhelming everything
that's worth noting.
I'm approaching appreciation and reconciliation of
mental anguish; can you complain?
It's not complicated if you want it when it comes to
dealing with yourself.
Just love it in the motion; just coasting,
soaking up the sun rays; don't forget the lotion. Look-a-
here.
I've been hurt before; you've been hurt before; we've
been hurt before.
Just passed the torch of love.

Day Tripping

For a while, I haven't been smiling,
as tears drop on the end of the page
as I write things down.
Distance and time made history.
So, for us, the old us can't be found.
All I know is to hold on to the goodness.
Afraid anxiety's coming to get me, moving as
I wish you were with me, praying,
"Dear Lord, please hold me down."
So…
I wrote you this letter
and tied it to a balloon
and I hope this letter
makes it to you very soon.

Older

As old as I am, I ain't got time for lies and bullshit; fussing,
two tears in a bucket.
Just came from the store to put something in the oven;
a full, good woman means loving.
Do the best I can, after that I don't give damn.
You don't know me; you hardly know yourself.
Telling me to uplift myself
to just push me to service just to service
those who service themselves?!
Bless you, or refer to the alternate.
You ain't the only one that can work yourself.
The best blessings are to truly know thyself.
How can you lead me if you can't lead yourself?
Tap into that internal/eternal fire that inspires your desire to
just try; as long as you don't lie to your inner light.
With warm delight, let the Earth give birth to the notion
everyone is important.
Good vibes are a worthy party outside.
As I sit here pondering, just posting on the porch.
It might be worth mentioning to you; presuming
my volume is loud, when actually,
I'm whispering.
Good gracious as long as you're listening.
Love goes a long way, that's why it's important

to take care of it before it's neglected and goes away.
Why put off today, start right away.

Imperfectly

I never perfected perfect.
I'm just imperfectly me;
just trying to find it out;
trying to figure it out; and
understand it; understand
things as far as I can see.
I'm just trying to figure it out.
I'm just a visitor for you.
I'm family to me.
I never claimed to be perfect.
I'm imperfectly me.
I may not have all the answers.
I just know that shit makes sense to me.

Love's Bad Luck

All I can tell you, babe,
dissing you ain't cool,
because in the long run,
I'm the one
looking like a fool.
So, I'm gonna
slip out and dip out the door. Fuck
all the bullshit issues. They seem
to last more.
One, two, three, four, five.
By my surprise,
issues too many to count.
Six, seven, eight, nine.
Receipts that are bona fide
at the bank of struggle love.
I know I ain't the only one
that opened up that damn account.

I'll Tell Ya

She worked at a casino.
She drove and lived in a Winnebago.
How I know?
She drove up at the laundromat
I was at.
Now listen,
because
I know so.
She was washing her clothes,
but then she
asked me
for a nickel.
I figured this was my chance.
I said, "Hello, baby.
My name is
Sir Pumpernickel."
She was wearing a white tank top
so I could easily see a nipple.
I said, "You want to go get
something to drink after this?"
She said, 'Yeah. Whatever it is
make mines a triple.'
Both showing thirsty signals.
Smiling, smoking on a salad.

So…entering in her garden,

you know,

I got to be fresh.

"If I told you,

that you captivated me

with your smile,

would you tell me your name?"

Our L's

Let's celebrate love;
let's celebrate life.
Let's celebrate us.
My rose petal love surrounded
with a lavender dream.
When did those feelings occur?
What was your initial reaction?
What was your instant reaction to me?
Where within that moment did you find love?
Of course,
your emotions are valid to me.
The only difference is
the course you want to go.
Let's celebrate the first step;
appreciate emotionally;
keeping us in the now.

Communication lingo.

Wanna Hear About It?

The only people that call me

are my woman and scam likely.

Between the two,

I'm trying to figure out

which one of them actually like me.

Let me tell you.

The 'Don't Tell Motel.'

A married couple cheating

on each other at the same motel;

adjacent rooms to each other

without the other knowing.

Competing sexual noise

versus sexual noise.

Not aware of the other

because they were supposed to be having

chicks' and dudes' night out.

Both unknowingly placing their hands

on the same spot on the wall for support.

Her as she rides;

him as he hits other coochie from the side.

Within moments, as if giving a high five,

subconsciously,

they still are touching the same spot on the wall.

Overall,

they both could have been together
chilling at a park, or on a bench
eating papaya, saying to each other,
"You're the one that I desire."
Instead, the dread behind the thin walls.
And yet, as spectators in the shadows,
we admire the silhouette
of their dismal future, full of upset pouty. The tale
of two counterparts in disdain.
As for now,
their selfish scenario is a private party.
Until both heard their familiar 'ooohs' plus one.
"Aye! Aye! Aye! Aye! Do I know you?!"
'Aye! Aye! Aye! Aye! Do I know you?!'
It depends on the words you choose, lovemaking, or
cheating?
"How dare you, ya' bastard?!"
Both thought they were being
cautious with their sacred promise.
It could have been really hardcore;
just being honest.

Been There Before

I've been constantly thinking about ...
Worrying; wondering if ....
Lost in such and such….
A symphonic arrangement of emotion.

Fickle Thing

What an eccentric and neurotic pair.
Our love, at times, can be a fickle thing.
'I love you-
then I hate you' emotions going like it ain't a thing.
It's like we're both committed
to being single, and our relationship
is just merely the fling.
You said so many things that day,
like I care who's listening anyway.
Some people in the world are fucked up.
Really you are just a pre-pay date away.
You're constantly wanting
a few more things.
Really.
I mean, you're begging;
let me tell you.
While a majority of the planet
is within individual highs,
my pockets are resting
and my patience are convalescing.

Honestly

I don't want
a gaslight-type of love affair. Sometimes,
relationships can be a sticky thing,
and sometimes communication
can make our feelings
feel prickly things.
Whether positive or negative
notice your relationships change.
The only difference is do y'all cultivate on,
or point fingers at?
Who is the blame?
Love is complicated.
What's the answer?
Maybe,
more of a question.
Do you really love me, babe?
Really love me?
Not the love above you.
Just the love next to you.
Never, neither of us underneath.
Do you really love me?

"Da Feels"

'Hey Monica!"

Monica replies, "Hey, back at you!

How was your weekend?"

'Oh, do you really want to know?"

I say with an anxious tone, but not wanting to offend.

"Yes!" Monica is glancing at me; her demeanor is,

'Thank you for the respect, but tell the damn story.'

"You've known me long enough to know if I didn't want

to know I wouldn't have asked a loaded question like that

at 8:30 on a Monday morning."

Blushing in my own right, I say,

"Remember me telling you about a lady

I've been talking to for a little bit?"

Monica replies, "Yeah, I remember;

you two have been talking

for about a week now; what's her name again?"

"Nora."

"Pretty name. Please continue," said Monica.

"Friday, when we got off work, I thought it was just gonna

be a single man's weekend not doing anything."

Monica replies,

"I was gonna call you anyway to see if you wanted to go to

the casino, but my ass left my damn phone here."

"That had to be brutal; not having your phone
for the weekend?" I ask.
"No, not really.
Sometimes you need to unplug."
"Please continue," says Monica.
"So, I went to the store, got some meat and poultry;
some charcoal; bottle of tequila---
you get the picture.
I'm at home in the yard,
turning over these succulent, tender chicken breasts,
and my phone starts to ring, and it's her."
"Nora?"
"Yeah.
She mentions she is in the neighborhood
and wants to know if it is cool to come over.
I'm like, 'Oh, yes!'"
"She comes over, and helps me finish grilling;
and she fixes the sides---
delicious is all I'm saying.
We're outside, listening to music,
while taking shots…
just chill'n until it got dark, and the mosquitoes
started being bothersome.
Then we came inside, cleaned up; and
finished the bottle, and played cards."
"Wait a minute.
This sounds sweet and all, but did you let her know
you were grilling?"
I reply,
"Unless she saw me at the grocery store
and didn't say anything, no." "Hmmm…continue."
"Well, it got to be around eleven or so, and she is wasted,
and she asks if she could spend the night; and I'm like cool.
I'm a gentleman, and say I will take the couch,
and she tells me that is nice

but I don't have to.
Thirty minutes pass, and she's asleep on the couch."
"I drape a blanket over her.
Crazy enough, we fart at the same time,
but she is still asleep; and I'm like cool because
I gotta go to the toilet anyway."
"I'd been cooking outside; I needed a shower.
So, while she sleeps,
I respectfully step in my bathroom;
do what I have to do; then enter the shower...."
"Hold up! She was that comfy?
She was just chilling asleep...?"
"On the couch."
"Did you put the shower head in your bathroom
like you were telling me last week?"
"Ooooh, not trying to go too much on a tangent,
but it comes with a pulsating mist,
and has a soft night light glow,
so you can shower in the dark.
They only had the clear shower curtains;
and it's just me so I don't care...."
Monica interrupts the story again.
"You really got my attention and
curiosity; so, it's okay to get in-depth.
The meeting doesn't start till ten."

"Well, back to the story.
The stream gave me a nice lather,
and slowly washes my body;
and the mist with the steam touching my skin
feels like I'm showering in the rain."
"I couldn't tell you how long I was in there.
The shower seduced me."
"All of a sudden, I start to hear clapping."
"Nora had been watching me wash for a while…"
"Wait…
What?!...
Hell naw!
How did it get there?! Tell it!"
Monica says, grinning with interest.
"Nora said she had got up to use
the bathroom, and heard the water going,
and she basically caught me pleasuring myself,
and she sat there and watched."
"You didn't lock the door?" asks Monica.
"I didn't think about it. I didn't feel intruded on or violated.
She had to go;
I was into myself, and she watched while she went.
"Clapping though…" says Monica. My response,

"She didn't want to startle me by flushing.
She waited until the show was over."
"Was it over?"
Monica asks.
"Nora took off her clothes and got in.
At this point,
 I'm more aroused than embarrassed as she watches me."
"She grabs my dick, and kisses me passionately."
"Then she takes my hand and places it on her open,
wet lips in a simple slow, circle motion.
Kissing on her earlobe.
I take my other hand, grab the bar of soap, and began
to lather her up providing kisses wherever she rinses."
"There is a moment within the moment
I didn't know if it was the shower or her."
"For a minute, I feel like I am swimming."
"She grabs my head just enough to still have
my tongue in play and she tells me,
'Get this throbbing pussy, and hit this fun box from the back!'
"I stood up, got a condom from the medicine cabinet,
and Monica if you were there......"

With intrigue she asks,
".... And if I was there?"
"What?" I reply.
"Well. That depends."
"On what?"
she asks, with an interesting look.
"Depends;
would you have left after she asked to spend the night,
or would you have stayed?"
-Two months later…-
Okay...
I'm in love with two women who are both equally magnificent.
I don't want to let them go.
Lucky me...
Why me...?
At least in my head it sounds selfish.
I could only imagine how you all view me at this moment.
Let's make this clear,
I never saw myself as a player; a ladies' man, or even Mr. Smoo
No, it's not about infidelity,or if one of them wasn't enough.
I'm just a single guythat's kinda cool and sort of a homebody.
So yes, even I don't have a clue.
The only thing I can do

is start from the beginning and maybe
somewhere it will make sense and mean more.
"I fell in love and I landed with a heartbreak.
Your love is more addictive than any hard-laced drug.
You're cheating heart got mine in a bad way.
I fell in love and I landed with a heartbreak."
-Three weeks after that...-
"Wait!
Ladies, at first, y'all playing and chasing, respectfully,
for me seemed kinda fun. I got the big head for a moment.
How I feel about both of you can't be
decided by random games
like love-me-nots, or shooting pool.
It's not fair; asking me to choose between you is like
choosing between eating or drinking.
Have my cake and eat it too?

That was never my intention....
What about you two...?

Yeah, this some messy shit,

but seems like I'm the most honest about my feelings.
Y'all played me and passed me around. Congratulations,
you showed us men that whatever we can do you can
do better; even with being jerks.

 Excuse me."

 I walked out the door; jumped in the ride, and left.

Perhaps

Maybe I do?
Maybe I don't?
Maybe I should?
Maybe I won't?
Why you playing with my emotions, pain,
and sorrow?
I've been rejected in many ways;
cold cut, deep fried fricasseed in a dusty cup.
Everyone around laughing and eating it up.
Tongue and cheek technique from your
grandstanding.
Lit the L
until it spelled leveled up; learning lesson.
As I continue to…
Keep leading the shake circus.
Bad chick circus.
Bright light circus.
I've washed my hands,
so, I proceed to the exit.
You a basic.
Peace and be cool.
For you, I no longer
need you to be in my presence
until tomorrow.
Then, emotions will be

drained for you.
My energy is hollowed like a tree.
Now it's time for me to leave and see
inspiration's landscape; imagination's showcase.
Let good vibes escape.
Spotlight Love.
Poems of dreams.

Shit I'll Tell Ya

"You don't want no romance,
you just wanna go and slow dance,
and spin around around,
dancing with your mirror image.
You just want attention,
with a glance of the possibilities rendering
of what you're missing. Whisper; tell me if
I asked you for a dance,
would you stay or let me pass?
Or,
do I even have to ask?
You don't want no romance,
you just want attention, and the glance?"
Before she could respond,
the DJ's call to action changed the pace.
"Ladies, if you want to groove,
get your tail up on the floor
and make your body move.
You looking good and let
the music soothe.
Get your ass on the floor."
As I musically make my move...
Don't you feel sexy.
Don't you feel sex-y.
Don't you feel sexy.
Don't you feel sex-y.

Sexy is what sexy is.
Sexy is as sexy, you
are you down to earth.
Sexy is you
still the brightest star...."
I yell out from my section,
"Aye!
Don't let them fool you, DJ bro!"
Pointing at this one,
"She said she wants a smart man
dumb enough to get with her...!"
She's like,
"Everybody wanna party and feel good.
You messed it up!
Now, my party vibe definitely messed up!
Aren't you lucky knowing I loved you, babe?
You lucky because you know I care;
but unfortunately,
I'm starting not to feel the same.
I'll get over it."
Looking at her I said,
"No, the fuck you didn't...!
It's on now!
I've been down too long, it's time to get up!
No, thank you, keep your
stress; I just emptied my cup.
Faith.
Hard work, with a little luck.
You may say who cares,
I don't really give a fuck,

but when it's you screaming it's unfair.
I'm financially stuck?
Just keeping it a buck.
Now what?"

Say There

Say-say there.
How are you doing over there?
Sexy lady, is it true?
Your interest in me has faded?
Is it true?
For you, a gentleman is overrated?
Actually; I'm the fool?
Being interested in knowing you was just a waste of time?
You hastily wanting me to go away?
Damn.
Okay.
I'll go away.
I would rather maintain
some cool moments while
I'm letting everything else go. Okay.
Perhaps I'm a sentimental fellow.
I don't know?
You just might hate me so.
If that's your feelings and notions, that's something
I would have never known.
Until now, I know.
So, if, 'this' ran its course,
I sincerely and humbly

take a bow, and travel a new path now;
your last chapter while you're my missed
pages from the ages of my book.

Drop Down

She trying to pop it;
fronting in front of friends.
Making statements like,
"Girl, yes!
He a mess.
My plaything's been
going crazy lately.
I am just insanely
tired of him calling my name.
All we do is scream,
then yell at each other again."
That's when I intervened,
'Forget you!
I should have holla at your friend.'

What They Want, "That"

The ladies say,
"We want that financially feel good ass money.
We want that family financially full ass money.
We want that scratch our
ass type of money.
We want that looking cozy,
never completely lazy, crazy
ass money."
What we all need and want
is to be safe and warm
against the storm.
We, the world really needs, Humanity!
Nice weather days,
enjoying one's own individual
ways that bring out the better in many ways.

Hit My Music

How you gonna sleep at night,
babe without me around?
It's like lost and found
with a smile turned around,
and a frown turned upside down,
and around and around again.
The poster chick of classy,
quite the contrary.
Negative, nasty and fake.
How much do you
want me to take?
Never ask a narcissistic mind,
that is a big mistake;
but she got mad at me
when she asked me.
I told her, "No," and she
tried to slap me.
So,
instead of getting mad
or saying gladly,
I threw up the peace sign
and jumped in the caddy.
I'm too old for bullshit
and
I'm too young for doing old tricks.

"You need to relax and breathe
in through your nostrils,
and exhale from your mouth.
Relax; close your eyes.
Relax; rotate your shoulders.
Five times moving forward
and five times moving back.
Don't come around asking me
if I've been to the liquor store.
When my car broke down and I
asked you for a ride, you said,
'Hell no.'
Talking about,
'I'mma kick back, watch TV, and drink and smoke.'
You could have had the decency
not to tell me so, you foul."

She Chimed Back

"I don't know about being rich, all I know
is that I met poor, and that, "fucka" is a bitch.
Listen.
As I walk you down to the corner store,
my liquor cost $5.00 when at first it was $2.34.
Betta pay attention, all this inflation got me itching.
Wait… is there something that
I'm missing?
Well, the doctor told me if I don't change my diet
my feet gone swell.
What the hell?"

Fool Heart

I'm a fool, but
let's keep it true.
I'm too old for games.
I'm giving you clues,
because I'm that dude.
You trying to put me
in a trick bag.
The treat is while you're
trying to put me in one,
you definitely stuck
in that same bag, too.
This ain't the sequel to,
"Bullshit part 2."
I never said that I
was squeaky clean.
(Moreso, a hopeful romantic.)
But I got feelings, too.
I took my L and moved on.
Matured; I'm cool;
in my own groove.
Dang.
I'm minding my business,
barbecuing these chickens,
and these ribs, amongst other thangs.
Please come around me with moral
intentions of good, and conversation of honesty.

For I have shared too many sad tales.
I got more than enough pain
that would drive most folks insane.
So, please stay in your lane.
I'll respect and do the same.
No one is the ruler of whom.
If you say,
"How dare you!" as an exclaim, remember
that's a revolving door, of course,
 I can state the same.

Same 'Ol

It's the same 'ol shit.
I said, it's the same 'ol shit just a different song.
Who wants bitter roses?
Over here!
We want bitter roses!
Are we here for love?
I need more than just someone good
enough just for the sake of taking pictures.
I need that love
I don't have to swipe.
Call me old-fashioned because I believe in passion.
Clearly old-fashioned;
are you into candles and conversations?
Creating dialogue so interesting and amazing,
unless I'm mistaking?
If that's truly you;
I need interest and conversation.
Now I'm having flashbacks!
It's the same 'ol shit.
I said, it's the same 'ol shit; just a different song.

Love for Sale

Once upon a time,
long, long time ago.
I was chill'n with smoke in the air.
Until I met this chick
walking on the stroll.
We were the same age,
but the night made her old.
Then she asked,
did I have any place to be or go?
 I said, "Yea."
'Then before you go
I got something to tell.'
"What's that?"
'I got love for sale.
Who wants bitter roses?
Love for sale.
Love for sale.'
She said, 'Be near me
at midnight.
Walking the stroll is hell, saying, 'Love for sale.'
Ain't gonna
catch me alone,
all out on a winding road.
'Love for sale'.'
She said for a little bit at a time she'd take me on a ride

'Love for sale.'
Show me things that
I never known.
'Love for sale.'
I said, "Baby,
I don't pay for what I get free
when I go home."
'Love for sale.'
She said she'd teach me things for a fee,
then a true freak I'll be.
'Love for sale.'
She won't leave me alone.
'Love for sale.'
'Love for sale.'
"Love is the payment.
Just love yourself.
Love yourself.
Love yourself.
Uplift yourself."
Time passesd.
Then she gave me
some money; I'm like;
"What the hell?!"
She said, 'Your conversation
kept me safe through the night.
All this time your
love was for sale.'

Banter Present

Do you speak for everyone?!
Up in here,
are you sure,
it's not just
your thoughts up in the air?!
You're acting like a
wine and double dutch competition.
If I actually can't find the words to say,
just know my feelings are there,
even though the important phrases
seem so far away.
Damn near nonexistent in a maze of bad days….

Party Y'all

I so glad y'all came through.

Party people in the house let me see you move.

You can skip, dip,

do whatever you wanna.

Do keep it cool,

don't disturb the party,

or ruin the groove.

Started in the evening,

lasting through midnight, and ending by noon.

Everybody wanna party.

We came to dance

our troubles away.

If you ain't come to party the exit is the other away.

The DJ's Inner Mission

Hey, sexy lady.
Hey, sexy lady.
Hey, sexy lady.
Hey, sexy lady.

Sexy lady, shake.
This the feel-good song.
Everybody sings.
I've been up.
I've been down.
In the middle.
Around the town.
Mostly walking about with a moody frown,
trying to find something
to turn it all around and around now.
I just wanna feel good.
I just wanna feel nice.
I just wanna have fun, so cool, is it alright?
I wanna dance with you, babe.
Hey, sexy lady.

Hey, sexy lady.
Hey, sexy lady.
Hey, sexy lady.
Sexy lady, shake;

underneath the stars.

Let's get
lost in
the rhythm
babe,
until we
don't
know
where we
are.
I just wanna feel good.
I just wanna feel nice.
I just wanna have fun, babe; so cool, it's alright.
Hey, sexy lady.

Hey, sexy lady.
Hey, sexy lady.
Hey, sexy lady.
Sexy lady, shake.
-Party people-

I'm gonna give you what you came for
since you walked in that door!

She Said That

"She came over to fuck."
'Say what?'
"I said, she came over to fuck!"
"She called and asked was I busy.
As the conversation's getting gritty;
peeking my interest really.
She said she wanted fuck."
"I felt lucky; in about fifty minutes.
it's gonna be me and some titties.
Much respect, give me a grown ass woman
who is confident; that's sexy and pretty."
"Besides, this love is crazy,
but the feeling so amazing; what shall I do?"
She asked me,
"'Would I like a taste of plum?'"
"Why, yes."
"Then the lady started riding my tongue.
I can tell she was a freak; we had so much fun.
This off the second, but because the first one was done."

Can You Match My Love?

It's not always about incense; cotton candy;
rose petal moments; feeling luxurious; perfect gumdrops;
forget me nots; it only matters how we face it
even if the faith in us drops.

Esmeralda's Parasol

-A Blues Song-

I was all alone at home, eating ramen; farting in the wind.
Call came in; it was Esmeralda with the powder parasol
"Sexy, how you been?"
She said,
'It's been a weekend season since we danced at all.
I was wondering, how within a week you and I
could do it all?'
"Esmeralda with powder parasol.
I have no time for the toxic life.
Esmeralda with powder parasol, I ain't got time to waste.
I ain't got time to waste.
I ain't got time to waste.
Did I mention?
I ain't got time to waste.
If you about that mess
get the hell up from my face."
"Esmeralda with powder parasol,
I'm just trying to relax in my space.
Messing with you means

going to the judge just to plead my case.
Toxic negativity ran up on me,
so they got a boot and some mace.
I'm cool, but listen to me when I say,
Esmeralda with powder parasol

I don't want to play, ya know?!
I ain't got time for all the bullshit
you trying to bring my way.

Esmeralda with powder parasol,

keep that bullshit away;
from toxic to negative;
keep that bullshit away from me.

How you gonna do something,
and say it was my fault?
Esmeralda with powder aqua parasol.

Go away from me."

Weirdo?

You don't believe in love.
Tell me, why should I even care?
I'm not your type because you
don't believe in love.
It's unfortunate.
Go ahead and label me a scrub.
My feelings are hurt,
but you're the one needing a hug.
You know that you don't really
like me.
Why do you want me to obsess; overstress?
You're toxic; not charming;
I find your disposition alarming.
Consider me lame because your type
is on another plane.
Two different planes; our landing logs

might be inconsistent.
I just cruise in my own lane.
It's a shame if manipulation
is the only game.
You know that just
means you were
wrong from the door;
beginning with stressful conditions.
Nevermind me, I listen to love songs.
So now what?
Go ahead,
label me emotional.
Weirdo?

Got Hip

Everybody, anybody; are you listening?
I can be upset with you, too,
spit venom like you, too.
Just for you;
suffer from chapped, dry coochie lips;
and your tongue has a taste of wet underarm pits.
Side effects fall to your ass;
shit tea lips;
tummy tucks, and facelifts.
You riding on my dick,
and I see you I eyeing my jacket.
Putting on it, it probably won't fit.
I got you from the basement.
Now you in the penthouse.
Yea babe, I keep my shit lit.
You expect me to pay all the bills,
and even your parents' shit.
You must be dismissed.
Checking my phone to see
if I got likes and clicks.
If I grab yours
you would trip and slip.
Mess around and break a hip.

Let your phone ring a little bit.
Be careful explaining that shit. Remember,
I'm returning back to you the best
collection of your greatest hits:
data; dates; and analytics.

Forgotten Cups

I picked you, so you're on my team.
I know I could text you with a ring.
You a ding-ding.
I know I could DM; that is true.
I'm a little bit old school.
I just want to talk to you
because you're so fucking cool.
Ring-a-ding!
Nothing wrong.
When I talk to you,
I smile.
Gonna give me that good, good conversation.
The world is turned upside down;
can't trust a smile.
The only comfort is wearing a frown.
We all trying to get through
the wild indoors, the jungle.
See how they can hinder you?
Wow!
If this the safe place, get me outside
these doors now!
It's raining on your head.
I told you to be nicer to people.
Despite the fact I'm wearing a frown,
you wanna make the world smile.
Ain't no one in love anymore.

It seems what's important are things bought from a store
Love songs ain't hitting no more; now rains are falling
down on the floor.
I should have put our relationship in a trash bag anyway
Mmm Mmm…
Why you looking at me like that?
What the fuck?
I feel fucking great.
I just fucking ate, and it tasted fucking great.
Ah, shit!
What the fuck you wanna do today?
I don't give a fuck; we're having fun today.
Hold up!
I'm fucking up.
I forgot the fucking cups.
I put the cooler in the fucking truck,
but I forgot the mutha fucking cups.

Not Prepared

I just flipped your hair.
I heard that you mad at me?
I got more kudos for your shit.
Just because you don't
believe in love doesn't
mean it don't exist.
Don't get used to staying and being down.
When you fall; you gotta get up.
The pressures of diamonds
can be so rough.
Don't keep putting yourself down when you fall.
Remember to get on up.
The pressures of diamonds can be so rough.
Please don't mistake the gentleman with a
chilled out pace with those who buy hoes
while ironing their capes.
There are times I can do it all by myself;
and there are sometimes I'm going to need some help.

I believe in giving good energy.
Only a chosen few share it back.
While looking at you back to front,
I'm trying to see my boo.
All I see is someone looking at me brand new.
You mad at the simple fact
we've been in toxic love;
I'm okay with that.

Lonely days, lonely nights.
Instead of fussing
and fighting with you,
ain't nothing new;
why don't we just break up,
I guess?
I'm not through free falling from a somersault.
I'm so scared of this love and you.

Struggle Love

Struggle love is all I know,
struggle love is all I show.
I was born out of struggle love;
if you got parents, you know
what I'm speaking of.
Surviving parents' old shit.
Emotionally spinning in this.
I leave from them and make
a life of my own; but struggle love
is the only thing
I'm programmed on, all day long.
I'm used to that struggle love.
When you see your reflection
who's looking back at you?
Is it the struggle love you've been running from?
Or,
is it when you look at your reflection who do you see?
Someone cool;
uniquely; extraordinary;
complicated; ordinary;
free spirited; spiritual.
Crazy; good; understood;
just amazing!?

Who do see?
Have you made up your mind?
Ain't messing with expressing how this sounds.
I am just trying to figure it out.
I'm not claiming to be perfect.
I'm just trying to figure it out.
"Can I share my low vibes to disturb your peace?"
'No!'
"Then quit disturbing mine!"
I'm not claiming to be perfect.
Just trying to figure it out.
I don't know.

Messy Note

Just sit back; just sit back;
now what a spectacle of a notation.
Monotonous dialogue; so open
and spacious, outrageous; good gracious,
Syncopation just did a backflip.
They're scared of love.
Without a drafted rhyme or reason, even believing
that the other one is wrong, and both correct.
Corrupt,
caught up on the wrong flow of paper mâché' roulette.
The weapon of choice?
Attraction's silhouette.
Step out or stay put, enough to see how jealousy looks.

Challenge 101

You just got challenged on the dance floor.
You just got challenged; who got that spot!
You just got challenged on the dance floor.
You just got challenged.
Who rocks the spot?
Calling all the party freaks; calling all the party freaks.
'Report on the dance floor.'
Calling all the party freaks; all in your face.
Ain't no need to sneak.
'Report on the dance floor.'
Party!
Move your body because that's what you came for;
 break it down; shake it up.
That's right, the crowd yelling out give us more.
The music bounces off the walls;
lingering through the door.
Everybody peep out the freaks
on the floor---check, freaks on the floor.
Break it down to the floor.
I hope your knees are really good;
can you bring it back slow?
Calling all the party freaks.
Calling all the party freaks,

'Report to the dance floor.'
You just got challenged
on the dance floor.
You just got challenged,
who got that spot!
You just got challenged

Take A Pic

Shake; get loose.
Show me more than you cute.
Shake it; get down.
Make a crowd.
Come around.
Take the picture.
Show me how sexy acts.
Take the picture.
Can I get your autograph?
While seeing you dance, hey babe,
I'm your biggest fan.
Listen to the intimate tango
of my materialistic love;
making your jewelry jangle.
In return, you can help me
make my jewelry jangle.
Question:
Can you handle this?
Can you run that?
Take the picture.

Liquify

Get your credit.
Get that money.
Use wisely with that cash;
if know your worth,
broke days won't ever last.
I've been searching.
I've been wondering.
I don't know, but
I've been working.
I would like to alleviate the
unchained majestic savage;
working hard; sunbathe in reverie,
with a radiant soothing exquisite,
sensuous, luscious alluring

recline of layback.

Dance Floor

I've seen her on the dance floor.

I want her to dance slow with me;

 just saying a few word to make

the moment with her last more.

"What kind of music you like?"

She said, 'Give me a lot; hardcore

funk me all the way down the hallway.

Kiss me with a ballad at the door.
Then, if I feel so inclined.

I might let you slow groove

me all the way to the floor.'

Then I said,

"To be honest, I wanna see you sweat.

So, when the party lights hit your body,

you start to glow more

 The breakdown tempo goes…

 Yet, I'm sitting at the party table;

I'm still at the party table.

 I'm sitting at the party table by myself; by myself.

 She took my body,

Then she left, walking to the dance floor.
She ain't hurting nobody; killing the crowd;
making them want more.
Got all the freaks clapping for some more now.
Working that body, damn!
Everybody reporting to the floor now.
Caution; sexy freaks on the dance floor now.
She had me spotted once I came in the door.
Who is sexy?
I just got to know.
She grabbed me. Consenting, she took my body;
got me thirsty, as of wanting more.
And the breakdown tempo goes…
Yet I'm sitting at the party table;
I'm still at the party table.
I'm sitting at the party tableby myself; by myself.
I'm just a wallflower

holding it up;
sitting at this table,
watching a few purses,
and a lot of cups.
I can't leave because
I'm watching everyone's stuff.
Now I'm stuck while she slow dancing
with someone else; fuck!
The breakdown tempo goes…
I'm sitting at the party table;
I'm still at the party table.
I'm sitting at the party tableby myself; by myself.

Que Sera

I need to hear the word to uplift my soul.
I need to put as much energy in myself
as I do for everyone else's
obligations, and unrealistic conversations.
What would I really like at this time?
To verbally unwind with cooler intellectuals, intrigued.
Honestly, this pain feels like an assembly line
on a belt that's constantly hitting with
troubles; and stipulation drift towards situation,
thinking back at start again.
That kicks off blizzards of insecurity;
mystically bad days.
I ain't mad, just statically scared of each other;
utterly more than I realized, your shoes placed upon me;
rain drops falling in snow.
Look at it.

Funk Me, Please

A parakeet asked a mockingbird,
"What's happening; where have you been?"

'Oh, I was just chilling; talking to some
turtledoves about four dirty hens
yelling and rolling in a bucket;
one spill out
the other three
said, 'Fuck it.'
Three dirty hens
rolling down the city;
one spilled out;
the other said,
'Tough titty.'
Two dirty hens
roll down to the market.
Only one came out, and
said, 'Damn!
He bought it!'
One dirty hen rolling
told the farmers to, 'Suck it!'
With an empty bucket;
the farmers had plucked it.
The turtle doves told the parakeet
'Fuck it!'
and took the bucket.'

Emotion Sensors

Like detection of heat signatures,
in the body like mood rings.
Wishing one night, upon the moonlight, cliché
teardrops fall from my mind.
I can't hide the rain from falling in my life.
Slow dancing among candlelight, swaying
to and fro in my puddle of tears,
stating when someone's happy; mad; et cetera;
I'll slow heal the pain into tomorrow.

Dark Clouds

It rains every day; sometimes,
it rains every day.
Mostly,
it rains every day;
or, is the rain every day simply in my mind?
It seems that
I've seen many storm clouds, wild winds run,
around and around;
teary eyes from rain come down.
I can't slip while down.
I got to get up somehow.

"At The Club Notion Noir"

We've all attended soirees that we couldn't ignore;
the hardship for any socialite in today's lavish nights.
Unlike the other nights of tired lavish, a single
wish from a birthday kiss sends a group
of women on a journey of a must escape.
The horror of rooms in a haunted escape room; lavish play.
The ladies have to get past a corridor challenge.
One is a double dutch challenge with metal formed as
chains instead of a standard rope; it
catches sparks as it hits the ground.
"Oh! Shit! I've seen this movie!"
One of the ladies,
whom is a drunken tag along of Janie,
the social leader of the, 'I'm Bored;
Entertain Me Crew,' waves it off and says,
"It's just jump rope, girl; go!"
Janie doesn't jump accurately
and it hits her ankle,
which makes her fall down in an endless corridor.
The remaining women go on.
"Oh, Shayla!" The drunken tagalong is the
new volunteer or cast-off
for the next challenge.
There is a sign that states one of the ladies

There is a sign that states one of the ladies
must sit in the spa chair with the correct button.
There are two spots to rest your ass,
but one of those spots will serve you patches.
As she is hesitating to sit down,
Shayla thinks, "I gotta piss now!"
Which one has the correct button that opens the next corridor?
If she chooses the wrong button, it's baby piranhas,
and she falls down a shitty shoot,
like being flushed down the toilet.
Lucky for this one, Cheyenne, cousin of the birthday girl, takes
Shayla's turn, and successfully makes it through the obstacle.
Then, Shayla looks at Cheyenne and the others
and says, "I've tried to hold it, but I gotta go to the bathroom!"
"What reality did you just realize this?!" Cheyenne states.
"The one where I gotta pee!"
They look each other with annoyance.
"I can't hold it and that's a motherfucking promise!"
grumbles Shayla.
"Get me the fuck outta here with Miss Tramp Stamp!"
hollers Cheyenne.
"Shayla, the only bathrooms we saw are from
the room we just left and
I'm not going back!"
"All of y'all characters can go back; but
I ain't got to go to the bathroom, especially with your drunk as
"Who did you come with anyway?"
'Janie!' The other women in the group tell Cheyenne.
"No; we gotta go girl!"
'No! I can't hold it!" replies Shayla.
'I'm going to the bathroom right now.'
"I don't know about that one," says Cheyenne.
'It's a bathroom; who cares what it could look like,'
 replies Shayla.

She goes to the bathroom,
choosing the one on the left as there are
two doors that say, 'Bathroom.'
'Oh! That's a big….!!!'
The door closes behind her.
Everyone's outside of the bathroom door.
Then, all of a sudden, it's quiet.
Cheyenne says, "I am not going in there!
One of y'all do it!
It's a bad day to go swimming outside fucking with me!
That's Earl's ex-girl; text him and have him check on it!
I have to go!
Now let's keep moving; she'll catch-up."
There is an X-rated movie theater called,
'Dirt Digger: The Return,' and 'A Hall of Mirrors.'
Three of the ladies say, "Fuck it; let it be so!"
and walk towards, 'Dirt Digger: The Return.'
As Cheyenne walks to,
'A Hall of Mirrors' with the rest of
the group, she responds,
"May it have clues!"
As the three ladies hold on to each other's hand, they sit
and wait for their fate in the theater.
One yells out, "I never learned to do anything!"
The light dims darker as the movie starts.
It's a gardening video about somebody actually taking
a hand tool and digging in the dirt.
They are telling the ladies about all the different ways to plant,
with a gardening tool being the only dirty hoe.
Neither lady is on that level, especially the ones headed to
the 'A Hall of Mirrors.' Cheyenne, for certain, looks in the mirror
with the other three ladies.

They are shocked seeing what appears to be an image of Janie,
the social leader of the, 'Entertain Me Crew,'
looking and pointing back at them,
while standing on a pedestal made of sand, shrieking,
"You saw what happened and you left me and waved it off!"
Cheyenne belts out; 'What happened to…?'
"The other ladies?
I made them sand for the time they wasted.
Either y'all just ugly, or y'all just see yourselves as monsters.
It shows that your attitudes are messed up
and y'all be forever stuck here with me!!!
Except for the one that said, "'Okay.'"
Cheyenne belts out in a heartfelt cry,
"My dear Rose!"
"I'm cool," says Rose.
"I saw some stuff, but I'm okay.
I didn't really see nothing…
the ones that saw the monsters
are so shaken they couldn't move."
"Yes, my sister is the one that stated she was okay,"
says Cheyenne to image in the mirror.
"Return to the party, and tell them," demands Janie.
The final door shows the exit that leads outside.
Before they went to the escape room,

the group of ladies were at a birthday party at a club.
They dissed the birthday party by claiming it was basic.
Poor Miss Every Day, who had one wish,
and that was to celebrate her birthday
with people that actually cared;
and for everyone else to fall in the despair of, 'She doesn't care.'
All except for Rose, who celebrated with Miss Every Day,
and gave her a gift just yesterday.
Janie, Shayla, Cheyenne, and the others at the party
played her off because there were no dudes with money,
or flashy thangs there.
The birthday lady was having fun
(even though she was ditched).
Now the birthday girl did find something else to do;
she danced with a guy that ended up being a millionaire.
Rose reentered the club twenty minutes before it closed,
and she took the party patrons through the aftermath
of what happened to her so-called friends.
Basically, the ladies should have just stayed
and kicked it with a friend at the club.
After they left the club, they could have gone
to a nearby diner to get some food, or until
somebody looked at their phone and said,

Fault False

Love, really you let me down.
Mistrust and bullshit, with
fuck you, and fuck your attitude.
You don't respect me; just guess
what I think of you.
Believe me, classy you're not.
Are you ready to gather yourself, and be gone?
I have little respect for and of you;
even responding, "Leave me alone,
and fuck you."

Ideology

In a world wind; when the room spins;
then you need to sit down.
Ideology is to see-through bullshit,
lying awake with unforsaken thoughts
from your sycophant's pedestal.
You need to slow down.
You asked me where I've been today.
I said, "I've been around."
You said, 'It's been lonely since you were away.'
I got a joke that was funny
You!
I would be considered mean if I felt it was true.
Both wearing a shirt saying,
'Feel sorry for poor lovely ass me.'
My dumb ass is in the other room.
Y'all know that I can't stand waiting up.
So, you were waiting; so funny, babe you are.
Remember when you told me,your ideology well
said? Returned back.

Too Late?

Am I too late?
Love is torn apart at the faults.
Both have dramas of time support;
speaking from my heart's conversation,
are now tournament debates
gone too far; this we can't escape.
Is it too late for my part?
Am I too late?

Sado's Pussy Cat

If y'all only seen this sado's cat; it's furry and plush,
I'm mean kinda fat.
Then, before I knew it, it was more than just a cat.
As a matter of fact, it instantly transformed.
As I turned my back, aww it's poised to attack
with the stance of a tigress.
So, if I run there will be no turning back; gotta chill,
I have to relax.
Where in the hell did she get that cat?
This sado's pussycat all in my face.
This sado's pussycat wants to run all over
my place as we speak now.
This sado's pussycat.
Aye!
Why don't ya wanna chill and calm down?
Damn.
This sado's pussycat a Lioness.
Only wants to control and run around.

Hold up, just as I blinked.
Oh, what?
This feline.
Oh, damn!
The truth, I must admit.
This sado's cat just turned into a
Saber tooth.
Oh, what am I to do?
Looking eye to eye,
this cat knew, and
permitted me to pet the sado's
pussy.
It's true!

She Told Me

She can take her clothes off easy,
but don't like to be emotionally naked.
She believes in love,
but her growing pains
don't like the rejections.
Then she said,
"It seemed smarter
to get money and attention."
Obviously, no objections.
Listening to her confession,
she said exactly what I was thinking.
'Without misconception,
just don't confuse
lust with good times
from the VIP section.'
Her reply,
"I need love.
Or, more so I expect it."
My reply,
'I believe in love so I respect it;
sitting on the porch.'

She Asked; I Got Condoms

She wants me to stick my tongue down her throat
while she's pulling aside her panties.
She's sexy, freaky, sultry, wet and sloppy.
Move that body, let me see that booty work.
Start from the front; turn you to the side;
hit the coochie from the back.
Admiring my work; we reposition,
feeling good as you ride on me.
Everything alright?
Sometimes, I do get excited.
Saying things like,
"Bring your booty cheek over here so,
I can bite it!"
"Slap me with a titty; seduce me, seduce me!"
"Come sip, sexy; for some hours, dance with me."
"Hold up!"
"You said you gonna make sure that my balls are emptied;
I said I'm gonna make sure your pussy gonna purr really
friendly."
"Give it to me now; give it to me now; give it to me now;
give it to me now!"
With both titties hanging out, fingering herself she said,
'I'm gonna give it to you now; about to shake the walls and
break the floor!'

I remember when we first met.
She didn't want a relationship to be one big regret.
"You don't have to hurt me in the process.
I'm really not the type to keep rolling around;

playing games like recess. Are we just…?"
I rebutted,
'Our lives may have taken us in two different directions.
You have always been the object of my affection.
You are way more than eye candy and an erection.
If anyone gives you any issues, remember;
I'm so cool you can hear me whistle,
walking down a dark alley with my guitar and my pistol.

To be honest it belonged to my pappy…'
As old sappy me continued the narration,
I got some other bullshit.
'Aye, I'll tell ya later.'
My woman is a stripper; her sister a stripper;

her cousin a stripper; her momma a stripper;

her auntie a stripper; and her grandma a stripper.
I'm so glad that I got with her.
Haters are so mad!
She butt ass naked and they still can't get with her.
Most dudes get with a stripper,
then down the line they begin to resent her.
All mad and bitter for the same reason why you got with her.
Now you in the mode to cheat.
Heard you were thirsty, fucking in the backseat
with the 74-year-old prostitute.
Freak not me!
She is my private dancer, she got a Ph.D.
She is just the neighborhood prancer to you, Sir.
Apparently, she got your money; so, apparently,
she found an answer.

On the Dresser

Standing by the car, getting some gas
I spy panties, crotchless.
A 50-year-old ass walking towards me.
Only a three-year age difference so it's cool.
As long as she doesn't get on my nerves or bore me.
Asking me what I knew betta?
So, I told her,
"I'd rather just leave it on the dresser."
'Damn!'
Left money on the dresser.
She want that high end; that vichyssoise;
she wants that everything,
no matter the cost.
"Yeah, babe.
I got money.
But I don't need that stressor.
I'd rather just leave it on the dresser.
Popping that shit all the time.
Damn!"
I met her at the gas station,
part-time substation, time waste,
trying to do some solicitation;
but trying not to make it a habit.

Tripping

What is every thang
without anything?
Like a turtle dreaming of a shell,
forgetting self, not feeling thangs,
everything got to get every thang.
Every time I think about you,
I think of a happy song; roses; hugs;
and tripping turtle doves created just for you;
just so classy, so nasty.
Screening all these DMs,
drop it to floor on a throne;
she's hot; just watch her.
They won't leave her alone.
Let the bass talk.
For me, I need not.
For you, you've been at this.
As long as you have me…
Never mind, this poem sounds crappy.

Don't Waste My Time

Precious is time; don't waste mine.
Don't waste my time.
I get stressed out while you
waste my time; don't!
That's why I don't think about you; you
kept on messing up my groove.
Don't waste my time.
Precious is time; don't waste mine.
Hey, you couldn't even keep promises.
Do my ears deceive me?
Starting off making promises
to me;
wanting me to follow you, and not speak.
You're weak, certified cheap.
You're basic.
Don't waste my time.
Precious is time; don't waste mine.

I Love to Like You

I would like to love you.
Even love to like you;
but would you even care?
Good days are approaching.
My intimate thoughts, you're holding my heart;
it ain't even fair to your heart; our hearts alone.
I loved you, but love didn't care.
Just to be clear,
how would I love, my Cherie?
We had a flare, let me be clear.

Sparking Conversation

Who took my lighter?
Time moving real slow sitting in my cubicle.
My woman gone and left me;
my dog gone and left me;
both named was Betsy.
Both couldn't wait for me to go!
So no,
I'm not gonna eat your pussy and then smile
just because I'm so far out,
and because women just let me.
Once upon a time, at any given time or place,
so delicious;
take a toke, just don't
choke, and cough on my smoke;
want more smoke;
want more smoke?
Don't ask no questions cause I'mma lie.
Still high off the conversations we've been on lately.
Have you ever been in love?
Have you ever wanted?
Have you ever been in the now?
Just contemplating, have you ever?
My dear, anywhere within a mental drift,
have us from this abyss with a mere uplift,
of your healing gift of humanity, lady with one kiss.
Then I shall replenish;
call me sensual.

I am the lyrical conductor
moving through your thighs.
Feel my vibe.
Who else would it be?
Who else could it be?
That you seek
'cause, uh….
Who in the hell took my lighter!?

Undivided Attention

I want your inner freak's undivided attention.
Picture it with in an instant.
Sharing drinks, we prepare for the night.
As the moonlight glares, you're tying down
your hair.
So tastefully wet,
for pleasure's affection.
So sexy we are.
While I'm sitting in this chair with an erection,
watching your wetness.
The selection of your clit and tits so delicious.
There's a place on my face for perfection.
You're so fucking sexy.
Even in an empty room
I can still get the proverbial floor messy;
intelligent and sexy.
What's the fuss

all about?

Let me see.

So sexy.

She's so sexy to me.

Let me tell y'all.

Everything all over.

So sexy to me.

Intellect on point;

so sweet and sexy to me.

More to me than

a fling, or an empty fantasy.

So sexy to me.

Consider me classy.

Expect me to be nasty.

An intellectual freak.

I'm just a gentleman from the hood.

Taking the time out respectfully;

to let you know lady, you are so sexy to me.

Silk and Lace

You felt you on you.
I felt me on me.
What does that mean?
We touched ourselves
in front of us
with so much love;
and longing lust
to exchange the touch of us.
Allow my seduction to entice your fantasy.
As the music begins to play,
sexy lady dance with me.
Entwined; embraced,
you elevate my senses
as you place a kiss on my face.
Liquid lady, may I have a taste?
Of your wet on my lips,
and your cream on my fingertips?
Oops.

I damn near forgot to mention:
don't make a mistake, I'm a freak.
Plus, I wanna spank you with silk and lace.
Indulging erotically,
and emotionally listening to my soliloquies;
physically, and spiritually, my third eye
sees that you're into me.
Passion, interest, and desires
for a beautiful scheme; a vision fascinating;
precious moments that are certainly cherished
and respected for this. I keep... Oops!
I damn near forgot to mention, don't make a mistake,
I'm a freak.
Plus, I wanna spank you with silk and lace.
Let's groove.
In your garden to dwell on sweet letters of words wrote;
reading a symphonic arrangement of emotions
spoke, gazing upon your eyes as you climax,
looking up in the sky as I drink upon intoxicating,

linguistic love; sticking out my tongue,
and to dine on your delicious clitoris
drenched in bliss; celebrate
your moaning with a kiss.
Oops.
I damn near forgot to mention,
don't make a mistake
I'm a freak.
Plus,
I wanna spank you
with silk and lace.

Wanna Funk

We are on our date night rendezvous.
All I want to do is be with you.
Softly tending in your garden,
my nature begins to harden.
If you blush,
oh, my pardon.
Having fun;
I simply don't care!
I got coochie juice
all in my hair.
After we shower,
we can go downstairs.
I got a notion that sped up
from slow motion.
I'm just coasting.
What's your urge?
While I'm swimming
in your valley, even near your alley,
I smell flowers;
tasting your pie
slowly in my mouth,
I lick and eat your upside-down cake.
What the funk you want?
Grab your back in the kitchen?
Keeping you reaching for shit

that ain't even there?
I, who swear when,
where, and why.
You are fucking with me?
It's just that.
I'm nastier
than you thought about,
with your panties moist.
All in the pillow case,
just thinking about hunching.

Pen Drifting

I'm gonna call this rhyme,
'Tammy.'
Because this beautiful, sick ass flow can't stand me.
Wait until you get a load of rhyme verses.
Wendy, Rochelle, Betsy, Erma, and Sandy.
What?!
No signal; you can't understand me.
Disconnected.
Damn, I guess you didn't pay attention.
By the way, I forgot to mention that,
'Know What I Forgot to Mention' is a song.
Magically, I'm in two places: the basement and the kitchen.
With my pen drifting, this next verse nasty, naked,
wearing one sock,
so bring back the lotion, lubricating your soul;
penetrating your mind; insert slow, smacking.
This big phat jiggly ass flow.
Got inspiration bouncing;
have you ever seen a muse on a pole?
Squirting out soliloquies?
No?!
I guess it's just me.
Sweating, making love to the rhyme like a porno.
With my pen drifting.
Inspiration like your pussy on my forehead;
touching the mental mind.
Going drip, drip, drip with erotic music soothing,
and tasty as a candy potion, while I got people listening.
Now just close your eyes and imagine looking at the sky.
With emotion pouring down like a tear of a raindrop;
puddle; pool creek; lake; river; sea;
or maybe it's an ocean of constant lyrical emotion.
From the other side of the tracks; loco but in motion,
my arms were dry; and nice lady offered me some lotion.
Never mind; in my lyrical mind, coasting.

Shy Blush

Intimate, intense; an enticing erotic bliss.
Our minds engage in a constant intellectual kiss.
Upon a moment, a waterfall pulses intrigue moisture.
I'm so clumsy I spilled my love upon thee.
Would you have been mad if I misted in your mouth
as you rub your middle finger across your lips?
Linguistics from my tongue grooves you, too.
The mood with the mentions of lowering your bra straps
made of music, as we dance within our gaze drawing closer.
Our lips immediately insist an audience; leaning closer
to the physical.

Personalities Vines

Depending upon the personalities,
love can be a jungle;
wild vines popping up everywhere;
over here and over there.
I swear I care,
nurturing all the flowers
to infuse the air
with love and cheer.
Oh, Dear,
you got a lot of pizazz
The world would be a lot calmer
if it had some grass.

Most News

There's gotta be a better way!
United we stand,
divided we fall.
It's gonna take all
to come together
to get through it all.
The whole world needs love;
and better communication
in all of our relationships.
I'm the frown turned upside down,
around and around.
The more we go,
I'm the frown
turned upside down,
around round and round
and round we go
round and round
and round
basically, trying to
find a way to understanding this shit.

Sometimes

What is left of a person who perseveres?
Is it the husk of time that has been weathered and torn?
Is it the stench of anxiety for moments spent anticipating?
Or, is it an echo of exhaustion
that constantly beckons for extra time when sleeping?
What is truly left is the journey of adversity,
with testimonials of peace.
In this demanding ass world, just relax and breath.
You have to get down to get up while telling
your troubles you don't give a fuck.
Sometimes.

Every Day Super

Call me Super every day.
My Super powers are getting up at 4:30 a.m.
to start my day, and staying awake.
Predicting the future of what to fix for dinner,
and I got a keen sense of what I like and hate.
Somebody get my cape.
I am your hero; on my way.
They call me
Super every day, every day.
On my way, aye,
I didn't fall from space.
I just take deep breathes
just to start my day.
I just was feeling blue.
Actually,
I need a nice space to create.
I'm sorry that I showed up late.
Somebody get my cape.
I bring good news;
you are Super every day too.

My Star

You are more than just a look.
You're my everything;
not just selfishly speaking,
you are the whole package.
Society's TV version of
sexy put ladies in groups.
Your unique style,
trend sets to be copied.
I've been smitten since back when.
I first met you in the lobby
and you told me your name.
All this time later,
I am still with you, babe.

No Secret

It's no secret that we make mistakes; it's a part of life.
Often, it's more common when you are younger.
Depending on the severity, you can learn from it and move on;
unless you're stuck haunted by past events as you get older.
Searching for a purpose; asking your inner self, "What is true?"
Do you dedicate yourself to follow the footsteps of whom?
Do you explore and enter wherever fate might choose?
Or, do you stay at home idle with nothing to do?

Effort

How we can make this love move so very far?
Are our imperfections our perfections?
My feelings are like
a slip of a banana peel;
commonly sub par.
From a word jumps into translate.
I'm up writing this in my sleep.
Working on timing conversations;
so amazing I couldn't help
but to be intrigued.
From more times we get better, I hope.
My feelings are slow pacing in conversation-less
stress, and in our situation.
I like romance nestled between a dream
upon reality.
Kissing on the very essence of your inner beauty.
Singing to our aura.

Changing Things

Let's go do something beautiful.
Let's craft a symphony to our hearts.
Let the woodwinds blow and harmonize.
Let the strings sing off just for a moment's whisper.
Let true love hit the door, while our
beating hearts provide the bass.
Is your love whole, or is it halfway?
Aye, tell me something fashionable
before the look gets ugly on our parts,
as I'm not perfect.
You get on my nerves.
Still, you are my lovely
sexy lady, Ms. Captivating;
the kindest; finest; baddest
intellectual.
Interacting with my eye caught looking for
a way to say, you are truly
the lady made for me;
forever and many metaphors.

Sensual Play

Can you hear the sensual symphony
of rhymes and soliloquies playing in tune?
A melody simply erotic to set the mood?
Cherry with Pineapple Peggy
looking from her sunglasses slightly pulled down.
Feel the vibes of songs flowering in bloom,
simply a catchphrase of love's
erotic rain made for you.
Wild, cool, bad, sweet,
when I'm down, you're lazy;
constant by your warm fuzzy greet.
Grabbing your cheeks, your sweet
hands stroke and mold my desire
to give upon you the best.
I'm going to show my chest.
I'm going to show my chest.
Are you gonna show your breasts?

Naughty

My rose petal, what do you want me to stimulate more,
your labia, or your vulva?
Tell me.
What will supercharge you like a nova?
Tell me.
What do
I supposed to say or do to capture
a tingling sensation from you?
Tell me. Place me in the direction you want me to go.
How dare you withhold this passion from yourself.
Naughty.
Or, am
I just tawdry with your emotions?
Like your love, your lust I must kiss.
Naughty.
You still want me, to play in between your enticement?
Naughty.
Nine different lips.

Are you for that; but you like it.

Thaw in Passion

Thou bosom aches with sensitivity after taunting
thy thick pussy with literature so tawdry
while scratching thine bum.
Lady, allow me to tickle your catastrophe.
Conjuring erection thrice!
I implore thee madam please beckon for my yard.

Good & Good

You got that good pussy.
You got that good pussy.
You got that good…
Gracious, wonderfully perfect.
Moist, delicate; I need to say more.
Front to the side, hit it from the back.
On the bed; couch; chair; or on the floor,
Move that wet pussy on my dick.
Slapping so passionately then
rubbing on your booty cheeks
as a thank you for allowing me
this bliss inside your flower.
I yearn for all of the delights that tonight has in store.
So delicious,
so juicy/gushy.
I don't give a damn
if it's trimmed or bushy.
I'm at perfection with my
lyrical and literal erection.
Putting in work.
Stroking like slow motion.
Your affection wet as the ocean.
Full throttle as our sex rocket pulsates.
As thoughts are gone in orgasm
right into outer space.

"Time and Attitude"

"Aye. Let me get two pints;
one dark, the other clear;
some wraps and a lighter."
Looking at the person he came in with,
he asks, "What you want?"
'Already got it. Let me get five scratch-offs;
you know I got you.'
While blowing him a kiss, she places a pack of nuts,
a chocolate bar, and soda on the counter.
"So," says the clerk, "How did y'all meet?"
Looking with puzzlement, "Oh, no!
We're neighbors,"
both say, laughing with mischievousness.
"What!? My apologies; I never meant to…"
"Well, darling sweets;
 Sparky got Dinky pregnant," she said.
"What the fuck! Oops!" the clerk replies.
"Y'all know what, I'mma just let y'all…"
said Sparky's owner.
They both laugh at the response.
"Wait, wait you want to hear this
 the answer though," he replies.
"Check this shit out. My dog,
 Sparky had jumped the fence to get some.

Then she came over to ask what I'm prepared to do."
"Well, I guess you can say after sixty-nine days,
Dinky and Sparky weren't the only ones hunching."
"Why yes," Dinky's owner blurts out;
"Dinky was going through pregnancy
while I was getting mine."
Looking at her neighbor laughing,
she abruptly changes the mood tempo and says,
"Fast forward; he said he was selling his house,
which he didn't initially tell me."
"That's because your ass's crazy," he claims.
"Fast forward. Like she said, we were fucking.
Then that, 'What the fuck we doing?'
started creeping in; and I just didn't
feel like dealing with shit."
"So, I did what the fuck she was talking about;
but I realized that I needed to be better than that."
"I went to her place with an anklet.
She looked at it, and placed her left foot
on top of the second step, and placed it
against her chin, slowly moving it downward,
from the front of her thighs to toes; giving me that,
'Ohhh that was sweet of you' look.
Then she gave a subtle smile.

I'm like okay…
Then she placed it back in her hand,
and took her foot from the steps.
Facing me, she dropped it towards the ground
with a flush of heartache and, really?!
I looked at her; then down at the anklet; then back at her
and said, 'I apparently know now how you truly feel.'
Turning around to my car;
I unlocked it; got in and drove off!"
"As he drove off, I did pick up the anklet;
and placed it in my shorts pocket," she replies.
'The anklet had a little key charm and, filler of story:
we were forming feelings, and working together to
figure out what to do; or who gets the dogs and puppies.
I found myself on my own mind trip, and stopped talking."
"One day after work,
I was going to meet up with my best friend
and her cousin for dinner.
Then, I just so happen to see him walking out
of the real estate agents' office with my best friend's cousin,
who ended up being his realtor."
"I tried to apologize, but he stopped me in mid-sentence,
and said 'I told ya ass, I don't want my heart apart
of any childish games!!!'"
Before, there were slight glances
of affection between the neighbors; now they were
gazing more at each other.

After paying for the snacks and stuff,
they left, laughing.
The clerk stood there for a moment,
then asked the next customer,
"What the fuck just happened?"

Age of Wine

Years and counting;
lovingly reaffirming.
They've been together, everything is good,
and today is their anniversary.
Sightseeing, looking at things near and far;
high and low, with new healthy perspective
mixed in with some aged weights
that are easier to carry, or let go.
Eating food's not just for the belly
but also for the spirit and mind.
Laughing not to conceal tears
but letting the tears flow for love and life.
Celebrating and dancing with growth and maturity.
As they go back to their hotel;
a conversation reviewing their past selves
occurred with sweet sentiment and slow prances.
After entering the luxurious room, and raiding the minibar,
they help each other with their clothes;
he's in a t-shirt and boxers; she's still wearing her slip.
They turn on the television, a pre-taped concert is on,
with their favorite artist playing their favorite songs.
They embrace, basically having fun in a dance.
A slight play of touches and moist passionate kisses.
From the lips of lovers' firework.

Speaker Park defined, created by Peter Cherry

A Letter to the Reader

Dear Reader,

Some people are loved and admired for their artwork.

Some people are hated and despised for their artwork.

Whether you're writing a sonnet, or building

a skyscraper everybody's tripping off your artwork.

You love me and you hate me for the artwork.

You are a skeptic and fanatic for the artwork;

appreciated, jilted, admired, foolish, loved, and

a genius, passionate for the artwork.

Captivated by creativity

 excruciating patience lately for the artwork.

 Thank you for reading.

Good vibes to you always.

Sincerely,

Peter Cherry

AUTHOR: Peter Cherry

Saint Louis, MO native Peter Cherry is an author, songwriter; producer, publisher, artist, and
co-founder of the musical group,
"KDLPC," with Kalisha D. Lemmitt-Cherry.
Establishing "Angelic Reign, Inc" publishing company in 2004
Associates Degree in Communications
from Florissant Valley Community College
Bachelor of Science in Media Studies
from the University of Missouri Saint Louis
Degree of the Master of Arts in Counseling
from Lindenwood University

Opportunity:
Capturing uncertain anxieties using black, white and grey tones.

IN TUNE:
Calm within the moment using black, white and grey tones.

t the Mud: Microphone Valley
e subtle influence of music using black, white and grey tones.